The Screams of War

THE ARAB LIST

AKRAM ALKATREB

The Screams of War

Selected Poems

TRANSLATED BY JONAS ELBOUSTY

LONDON NEW YORK CALCUTTA

Seagull Books, 2024

Original text © Akram Alkatreb, 2024
English translation © Jonas Elbousty, 2024

ISBN   978 1 80309 350 5

British Library Cataloguing-in-Publication Data
A catalogue record for this book is available from the British Library

Typeset by Seagull Books, Calcutta, India
Printed and bound in USA by Integrated Books International

To the Syrian people

CONTENTS

AMERICA'S POEMS

TRANSLATOR'S ACKNOWLEDGEMENTS

I'm immensely grateful to Afaf Tamim, Karima Belghiti, Yazeed Mualla, and the anonymous reviewers for reading this work and offering substantial feedback. Likewise, I'm deeply thankful to the editors at Seagull Books for their invaluable feedback and assistance throughout this process.

Akram Alkatreb was born in 1966 in Salamiyah, Syria. Thereafter his family moved to the city of Homs, situated in the middle of western Syria, where he lived for twelve years before moving back to Salamiyah, a city from which hail prominent poets such as Suleiman Awad, Muhammad al-Maghout, Ali al-Jundi, Fayez Khaddour and Ismail Amoud. After finishing high school, Alkatreb moved to Damascus to study law and earned a bachelor's degree. However, his passion since an early age was—and still is—writing. Thus, he has never pursued a career in law. Instead, most of his time in Syria, in particular Damascus, was dedicated to creative writing.

In addition to being a poet, Alkatreb is a literary critic and journalist; his pieces have been published in prominent literary magazines and newspapers in the Levant such as *al-Nahār, al-Ṣafīr, al-ʿArab, Nawafid, al-Hayat* and *al-Mulhaq*. Many Syrian writers of his time published their work in Lebanon to avoid both institutional censorship as well as possible repercussions of their publications under the Hafez al-Assad regime (1971–2000). Alkatreb was no exception, but he was often courageously critical of the oppressive tactics of the regime, which included censorship, imprisonment, writers' cooptation and the dismissal of the writers' union. He was one of the signatories of the 'Statement of 99' (September 2000), in which Syrian intellectuals called for the freedom of speech, press and the release of political prisoners, among other demands. In 1996, Alkatreb was invited to visit the United States as a writer and poet under the International Visitors Program. He visited several universities, including Georgetown University in Washington DC and the University of Texas at Austin, where he gave lectures about Syrian poetry to students in Middle East Studies departments. In 2001, he settled in New Jersey—not as a visitor but as an immigrant, joining his wife, who had immigrated a year before his first visit.

Alkatreb began writing poetry at an early age, and his first poem was written in middle school, dedicated to a girl he liked. However, he remained reticent about the exercise of writing when he was young until his brother discovered his dairies—a personal anecdote Alkatreb shared with me. This early love for composing poetry blossomed into a successful writing career. He is the author of half a dozen poetry collections; some of his poems have been translated into Spanish, French and English. The present volume is a selection of poems from four of his poetry collections: *Musammar ila a-nawm k-ibn wahīd* (Nailed to sleep like an only child; 2003), *Qasā'ed amrika* (America's poems; 2007), *Bilād siriyya* (From a secret country; 2013), and *Kitab al-gharīq* (The book of the drowned; 2016). Spanning nearly a decade and a half, these poems chronicle a significant portion of the poet's life and trace the development of a noteworthy literary career.

Throughout this volume, the themes of exile and nostalgia are at the centre of Alkatreb's poetry. Longing for the past in familiar landscapes contrasted with life in a new world with all its eeriness, newness and (dis)comfort take a pivotal role, of which some of the poems herein serve as unequivocal testimony. These 62 poems depict the poet's formative years in Syria, his experiences in exile in the United States and his persistent longing for a past rich with memories. The poems vividly portray the well-trodden terrains of the poet's life, such as his house, neighbourhood, schools and interactions with siblings and friends, as well as nostalgic walks through the alleys of Damascus. Alkatreb provides a comprehensive picture of his life in both Syria and New Jersey. The poem 'Syria' opens with the geographical separation between the poet and his homeland: 'Once only a few miles away / now thousands apart'. Through a vivid metaphor, he goes on to offer an image of the impact of conflict that has consumed his beloved homeland: 'and the bird breasts glimmering on coals / like the planet Venus'.

Poems such as 'Freedom' narrate the catastrophe of war and how Syrian lives have been imprisoned first by the Assads' authoritarian regimes and later by the Civil War. The reader witnesses despair and loss of homeland; Syria is ill-fated, doomed to remain 'burning'. Through harrowing verse after verse, Alkatreb lays bare the searing agony of his world. Each poem delves into the most brutal scars of war, a gut-wrenching testament to the devastation it leaves behind. The title poem itself—'The Screams of War'—speaks volumes of the poet's painful exile, a witness to the destruction of his homeland. His voice, steeped in despair, narrates the unfolding catastrophe. Alkatreb's birthplace, Salamiyah, is reduced to rubble; al-Khalidiya, his childhood haven, is no more. The buildings that cradled his youth stand in shattered fragments, silent ghosts of a ravaged past.

In 'Here and There', the poem's title immediately captures the geographical and physical distance between the poet, who lives in New Jersey, and his mother, who is in Syria. Alkatreb continues to reminisce: 'I reminded her of the past, the trees, and the rooftops'. This yearning for the past reverberates in many of the poems in this volume, including 'The History of Emotion' and 'The Street of Hymns', among others.

The Screams of War is a visceral collection of poems that confront the realities of contemporary Syria. Akram Alkatreb's verses capture the sense of the quotidian during war. His words, 'murmurs engraved on stones', long for and despair over an irrevocable past. At the heart of Alkatreb's work lies a preoccupation with trauma and the profound burden of alienation that accompanies exile. Nascent memories are shrouded by the 'scars of sleep' and the ubiquity of violence that he channels into his poetry does not tolerate enclaves of innocence. *The Screams of War* is an unforgettable testament to the resilience of the human spirit and a stark reminder of the harsh realities faced by those trapped in conflict.

Jonas Elbousty
London, 20 December 2023

NAILED TO SLEEP LIKE AN ONLY CHILD

TO AMAD

I am a stranger to your mother's family,
I am the living dead.

Stare at me with your skies,
with a trembling scream under the wind.
Carry me with your gaze just the way you are,
give me what makes me a learning paper
like the violin to your right, there
my heart opens like a broken umbrella.
My charred touch, next to you, all night long,
dew emanating from your steps, just the way you like it,
while you burn around me
all this sleep
I am that voiceless syllable under your tongue
silent and sad
like a rhinoceros.

THE IDEA OF GOLD AND THE RELEASE OF THE WIND

I.

For you, I am allying with the flames
—your hand in mine; sofas and night squeaks.
—the partner of your steps partners with what is next
the fire's motherhood.

There, I stay up late next to your shadow, to wash
your feet with thunders and the wings of the hawk,
then I caress
your face, thinking of gold
and the release of the wind.

Busy with your subjects who are enchained to the illusion
        of your light,
they insert their accents like tobacco rolls
under your chair.

I apologize to your coat, to his sleep on the fan:
To bite the day like it was a pistachio,
and I need to stand, drunk, in front of
your disciples, misleading my route to you with a
        volatile fate
white above fishermen's fights—among them are those who
keep busy biting their nails—amazed by the final scene

At the sight of my blood
leaning towards your name

And just like the carrier of feelings, I lighten my demise
    with you:
—I have two slanting shoulders.

Abyss
burning
like the eyes of Bedouins
while they slaughter their only horse
for the stranger.

II.

Your voice is white
like a hand poured on the night

III.

Between your trees
I followed the traces of my blood
there . . .

I found the moon
singular like a scream
sleeping in the heart of a stone.

IV.

Your smell fills the space
God's subject in the old books.

V.

Only the light
a man on the edge of the shadow
fallen on his face.

I.

To Janset . . .

Like that:
With almost a match
your flowers can leave my heart
while screaming:

—Where are you, until now,
the dusk arc and the tents?
You are one of the doors
knocked by the tongue
and the sound
the rattle of the hands.

II.

In your thick water
next to you:

My body turned to a bed,
a scream on the edge of a hill
and dead horses in the bushes.

The maker of birds in his blood vessel.

III.

Nothing makes me hesitant
while my son is sleeping in your veins

Waiting for me to come
to your tear like any broken vehicle
barely seen.

IV.

On the page of my life,
I feel your reflection like a thousand rings,
or the imagination of wandering tribes

I raised in your flesh more than one tear,
and ashes wiped the damage.

The tremor of horses,
progenies without a trace.

V.

I love you
as if I were lost in the lines of your palm,
they show the movement of lost stars
on top of your stained shirt
in white and black

Stars stolen from carts,
zinc plates,
pages of features,
slowly milled.

VI.

I bow to your scent.
I wave to the drowning who lean
on a straw when I tell you:

—I am not that much dead,
especially in front of the mirror where we left
our necks,
our cut ages,
our heritage,
there is no salvation in desires to ooze
just like a deep wound.

VII.

For a hundred years
I get older with each of your breaths
tied to the nod of your touch and the view
of your shadow left out for a while
near the chair,
absent-minded.

For a hundred years
I am lost around your hand's gesture:

—like a sleepwalker to epilepsy
and the moment in which the horses bathe
chained to nudity.

—like a walker naked,
dim,
confident in the closure of the path.

BLESSED BE WHOEVER APPROVES YOUR NAME

I.

With a bird breathing between the lines,
and with a cloud almost emerging from the index finger,
I am writing to you about a deserted continent
near a port,
a wooden ladder
upon which God stands to look
at my
heart:

—Blessed be whoever approves of your name when they
    cry over the cypress,
for when the night passes by your rose,
for your mercy that takes me to the wind blowing from
    my right.

—Blessed while I pass by your house
gifting you a name inspired by the rain.

What discussions do we scatter at the entrance to the
    garden . . . ?
With the power of the shadow,
and the will to stand for the bare trees,
we realize how old the wind is under our flesh,
lit by the lanterns near the movement of your name,
I memorize it by heart,

without the guard stepping forward to apologize,
or to rearrange my mind as it wanders for you on the seat.

The end of the era
your hand digs a salute in the corridor
which counts
the traces of my days on your clothes:

—With a little hesitation, I prepare
what befits from the flames,
light as the humour on a slow train,
and white.

—On a lot of days
I wish I could live all at once
to know where I was through all that oversight.
In your closet . . . ?
Or between your books which whimper
at the few flowers of mine?

Here I am on the steps of your life,
raising for you enamoured children
with dusk and balconies,
they come from faraway mountains
like rivers kicked out from their families,
growing up to be like the storms under my shirt.

Now I want to take care of you,
to sum up, loving you is like watching
the confusion of birds.

II.

I am bringing back to your name the features of the
    stateless eyes,
and to the uncovered roofs, under the piano of darkness,
the meaning of the buried spirit on the stone.

Cords, to your scent, white,
statues of tears,
intentions, like marble, blind on the cliffs.

Your step is a light murmur
thrown on the floor,
your step, the granddaughter of the moon's light,

Is trying to lose weight.

My leaning sadness is like a sunflower
sticking to your clothes.

The water is for you
so we can go back to your breathing hand
on the burned shoulder.

PHOTOGRAPHS

—like a fallen syllable from the tongue.
—a face pierced with a dead glance.
—like one hundred strangers dying.
—he comes out of his photograph.
—those who are sure they will die.
—my father.
—nailed to his sleep like an only son.
—the grabbing of the gun.
—the statues in the afternoon.
—the angel made of bronze.
—the daughter of the river.
—a painting in black and red for Fateh al-Moudarres*
—walking with a cane.

* Twentieth-century Syrian painter, one of the leaders of the modern
art movement in Syria.

We rubbed off the thirties
while leaning on the clothes
from which we filtered
lost grandchildren with our breaths,
disappointed with the walls
and the screams portrayed in the angles of the ruins.

We rubbed off the thirties
with miens that barely look lonely
and indifferent eyes

Less mysterious than the horse's tears,
wider than a hand
trembling like an ivy leaf.

We rubbed off the thirties, when suddenly
we couldn't discern that body imprisoned
in a hole:
—Our life, storming
like
a slip
of the tongue.

A FACE PENETRATED BY A DEADLY GAZE

I.

Like when the wolves howl on the brick slab
we go
shaking like suspects:
— They are describing the wind
while they are dead.

* * *

II.

The cruellest thing about dawn:
the manuscript of the exodus
torn up by a distressed wolf
because of the night's death.

III.

A face penetrated by a deadly gaze.

* * *

IV.

The bird in the blueness
a printed step on the sand.

* * *

V.

Wolves counting their howls
inside the eye of the well
the bleating of surrendering herds.

* * *

VI.

Under our feet, the stones shine
like ancient gold:

—O wind!
Let us talk together, without a blink of an eye,
or walk on the water,
as though it is a broken piece of wood.

Blood on his back
blood, the fighters' law,
he steals it eagerly, with the feelings of an orphan.

'Someday, we'll lose him'
that's what a woman said
she was standing near a coffee-shop door in Latirna.

Like a few breaths
on the afternoon line,
he's falling like a drawing
dead with the charcoal pen,
leaving behind him
all that shakes under the sun of God.

Like that:
like one hundred strangers dying,
surrounded by aches of bodies,
an obedient gaze
in a wounded land
with thirst.

The man in the picture
will not leave
before he bombs the shadow's life.

He cauterizes the country's flesh with the family's merits,
and the touch of blood,
and the books that praise him for reaching ninety.

That man who carries us in his smile
and in the stamps that bear his likeness
leans over our houses
with a coat of wrinkles.
He is blessing the way we walk
and circle around the statues of the sons.

The man is overturned like a ladder that
creaks like a grim afternoon
extended above faces
while moaning like the beggar's charity:

He is rising from his photograph
while sleeping alone.

THOSE WHO BELIEVE THEY ARE DEAD

Those who are certain of their death
and of air under the stones
darken the sunflowers that lean
on the cliffs accosted
by excessive looks.

Those who believe in the scar of sleep
—the generosity of ruins—
the jinxed names
the casualties from darkness stuck on the back of the world.

The features are reflected
in the release of tears.

Those who believe in the currency of patience
were burned out in the alleyway.

And without any notice,
they came carrying barrenness in their demeanour,
the pedal of clipped shadows under their eyelids,
the calendar of regret,
leaning next to their silhouettes like broken doors.

On the doorsteps,
they broke the window of insomnia.

Those who believe in the easy eclipse
and in their perished lives
in the annexe of void,
and the page of the white thieves.

They came early to their death
with hoarseness and a sand clock.

MY FATHER

I.

The one we left on his door
half god-leaning,
only he knows
that his life is a straw bundle
and his three children

Like stickers
on the wall of his old body

He, at whose door we erroneously left
half a tear
and the wire of a defunct phone,
names of towns not traced on a map,
forged currencies,
and letters we've been writing from the neighbouring street

to him we returned silently with a cart full of laughter and
    bruised blood.

II.

My father
the one who sold, without mercy,
a third of his lands,

to make me at the end
a respected man of law

He did not see me later on
when I turned my back
on Hammurabi
and Thomas Aquinas
and on the volumes of dust.

My father
the one who put a mortgage on his house
and cried every summer
so I can rent, in the capital's downtown,
something like a room
or even a brick staircase.

to him I returned a poet
and 'a criminal by birth'.

I.

Stabbed from behind,
the wanderer's back collapses
like an old windmill.

Stabbed by the increasing cold,
on his shoulders
a loose tear
with no clan or a country to call home.

Nailed to sleep
like an only child.

II.

All that they did
was lightly waste their days
and flirt with the hatred hanging gently from their faces.

They left their voices in the blue well
moaning like gledes.
and on the terrace
they forgot the doorknobs,
the looks,
and the crying fits.

All they did
was not remember.

III.

He was conversing with his hands
like someone running away from demise.

He's the one who saw
an angel dragged by the dead flesh eaters,
they already named him the towering door—
the moon's prophet!

IV.

The warriors lost their way at dawn because of her,
carrying on their shoulders what tempt the kingdoms
while the villages sigh.

Wounded men with strange accents:

They mounted her bread with the smell of their bodies,
then they left—suddenly—guarding
the cracks of the houses, stammering and barefoot.

The shadow of her gaze
is death in a faraway land.

THE PISTOL'S GRIP

On the table
the pistol's grip is shining
between one step and another,
nothing prevents me from touching its nozzle,
and the trigger that waits for the zero hour.

Between the door and the entrance to the bedroom
there is a body lying like an anchor on the sofa—
it does not turn its head
nor glimpse across the threshold.

THE STATUES OF MIDDAY

My friends are the brothers of darkness,
statues of midday,
nothing left from their features
beside the smell of the hand extended to the waiter
behind the coffee shop's window.

A harsh hand, frozen from the cold,
flaunting,
or blinking like a tearful eye.

Without being lonely,
the Hudson looks like a secret manuscript
weeping from the weight of the drowned.

A black and blind man is turning around,
as if at the edge of an abyss,
alone at the edge of his body leaning by his musical
instrument,
eyes closed,
floating like an angel made of bronze.

FROM A SECRET COUNTRY

SPARTAN'S WEDDING

Once on Orontes's bridge
there where horses bathe as if they were going to a
    Spartan's wedding
while many pieces of clothing hang on the trees
boys swim in the green water
holding sweets and pieces of bread, laughing

In the evening, one of them will be carried away in a
    stretcher
his complexion mirroring the river's colour . . .

I am thinking, for example, that we take a taxi
and hide in the mountain near Ibn Arabi's shrine.

The photographers want to seize from your time a
    moment to capture a photo of you on
the road to Damascus
while your children are waiting for you in the house of
    John the Baptist:
here where a whole life is being lived for an angel from
    the Middle Ages.

At that time
in that place where the wounds are taller than the stones
and where wings grow on people

I want to reach you barefoot
and I do not have enough money for the road.

Cut from a leaning tree in front of your house.

I want to run back to being twenty-one years old
because I am unable to forget the scent of your body
in the city of the blind . . .

A BUST

This Syrian face—all you can do is take it back
to the watercolours of Cézanne.

It is beautiful to be a bust without any doubts, it is
    undamaged
and the stars never leave its eyes
so it looks like an ingenious sentence in an old Egyptian
    tablet . . .

A SOLITARY TREE

This man who stands full of life and does not easily
    surrender himself
performs his historic dance and weeps with fish

All that surrounds him:
wounded humans in front of houses,
and a solitary tree.

I did not mean to hurt you while you were dying for me

I am waiting for you like a Circassian dreaming about a
    mat under the sun of the Caucasus

or an Armenian longing and searching for Mount Ararat
    from the train window in Hejaz station

or a Palestinian from the diaspora reading the novel
    The Sun Door from a balcony in the Yarmouk
    refugee camp

or a Kurdish playing all the sad songs of God on a
    buzuq.

I am waiting for you and my eyes are shot . . .

How can I reach puberty while I am running towards you
a little drunk, and all this blood that I cannot describe
even in an evil life.

Your excessively written body has the weirdness of little tricks,
lots of *A Thousand and One Syrian Nights*,
and the prolific crescent is an uncovered book . . .

Her mouth that resembles the screams of war
those who fall, the dawn in their head
a bird with two wings . . .

Every day that passes is a sigh in front of your locked door.

Your trembling mouth is charming the men who head to war,
meanwhile I cannot stop seeing your face all night long
like I am seventeen . . .

In the city of the god of Sun
hands in the streets drawing God sad like the village
    children
as they wait for the cloud to arrive, carried on the backs
    of sheep.

The great mother sleeps, her head uncovered:
her body is the bread of offering
her body that is suffering . . .

The jerks do not have any honour
they do not have your name that is carried to the
    prairies on the backs of horses
meanwhile, the sons of violence take you to spray
    perfume on you
before anyone notices the trees of God
that are rising from the blood . . . .

I WANT TO UNHURRIEDLY DREAM ABOUT YOU

Syria that I yearn for
Put your long war aside under the shade of a tree
I want to unhurriedly dream about you
without shedding a single tear . . .

SYRIA

Once only a few miles away,
now thousands apart.
The door ajar,
the alleyways,
and the bird breasts glimmering on coals
like the planet Venus.

To the handler of greatness

Do you think this summer will ever end,
the pole star that still resembles the European pear
tottering at the summit of Mount Qasioun?

That beautiful woman there,
the one who was sitting on the wooden chair,
could not make me forget the face of Damascus from a
    short distance
while you are reading about the invaders and *Labyrinths*
    by Borges
and the saints wandering on their faces . . .

FREEDOM

The bird that we lost
on the edges of the prairies and the cliffs . . .

We are your sons, and we are leaving the world.
Do you know how much we love you
and that you are about to die?
Your body was hanging in the air for ten thousand years.
Are you still alive?

So we can meet by chance in the history books
that praise kings from the Stone Age?
Then you lose your birds, your soul, your trees, and your
    mother tongue.
Do you know how much we love you?

BOOK OF THE DROWNED

POPPY FLOWERS

One of us can risk his life
when the day is complete

With this easy vow
in the Mayan tribes' country of origin
the poppy flowers are withering secretly
and on the rocking chair
composing curses leisurely
soon we will reach old age without a speaker
or the knives hung in the corner of the kitchen.

One of us can cry nonstop like a slaughtered animal
and in the pure scene in which the seed of evil squeaks
we discover the smell of the dung
and the secret word for oblivion.

There are the ships from which mysterious people are
    disembarking.
You beg them so the dawn doesn't appear from behind
    the mountains.
They enter your house and never leave it.
Then leave an Assyrian note on top of your bed,
hence you awake leisurely without the risk of your
    shadow falling off.
Meanwhile, the historians are writing the history of
    hugging that the city never knew,
the nomads never mentioned it in the books, nor did the
    museum lovers,
until they saw your naked statue from behind the glass
    in the Louvre:

They cry at your small feet.
They cry your winged horse
and the movement of your clouds in a book placed
    under the bridge.

And the name of fighters who left roses in villages
then went to sleep near the Milky Way:

They're raising their hands to touch every part of you
making the tree flood with milk.

I left all of Damascus at your door.
The moon will not rise on the roofs, for the children of
    my neighbourhood are laying grapes
under the August sun,
then they take you to their dreams.

I must wait another twenty years to teach them the
    lesson of regret.

Each of us wants to steal your heartbreak.
We desire you like we desire the bread sold in front of
    shops.
And we follow the smell of your robe, which reveals
    your breasts in front of the children,
transforming them into trees and sunflowers.

You are taking off the buttons of the springs, and with a
    parched mouth
we run towards you to discover the origin of writing
    and of reading,
and we try to sleep next to you in bed
but your lover does not want us in the house.

The balcony
for the body to transform
into the smell of coffee beans.

The body
for the balcony to transform
into a trace of a wing.

The balcony and the body
for the shadow to become blood and flesh.

About that gutted, forlorn place,
and about the body that could not break apart
and your taste in the bread and salt.

And all that holy tar that flows into the rivers,
and those who travel far and long
in order to descend from your dynasty.

And they only ask about peace
and about a simple balance in the unknown bank.

All that blood that is flooding the television and the
    diesel motors
was never enough to raise a scream
it made the utopian poet write a sentence about the
    naked humans:
they die and their souls rest until the end of the night
like trees from faraway fields.

GEOGRAPHY

This place is an old, exhausted home country,
we're waiting for your clothes to dry on the line
but no wind comes,
we're sighing, which makes the cypresses grow,
they're just like the people praying

with murmurs engraved on stones,
we compare you to gloom.

BETWEEN ALEPPO AND MOSUL

Every time your eyes lay on them
they secretly lose their names and their children
along the closed road
between Aleppo and Mosul,
where the darkness is the head of the family.

Once upon a time, they had this habit
of roaming around you from a mile's distance
before they went to sleep.

These are the walls of the houses on which I drew
trees and birds
and a river that crosses between houses
in which children drown at night.

The street that we used to cross between Al Baramkeh,
Bab Moussalla and the old Zahra Road
takes you to Cité Ettadhamen, like when I was that age
in that charred era,
I was pointing to a place from the bus window, and we
were humans that looked like the dead from ocean
graveyards
crowded inside it like statues in unbuttoned shirts.

It was enough for me to find the house key on top of the
electricity meter
at
the time
when
darkness
invaded
the city.

The most important things that were forgotten are
    those stairs that no one discovered
those annals sleeping under the skin
annals of the power of one man to transform a
    whole nation
to a generation thrown into the middle of the desert.

A hand that had not dried up yet
shakingly turning on a lightbulb,
throwing the shirt on the edge of the bed
and shedding tears from satin.

Just a hand
slapping the cheek like an upturned vehicle
then asking for forgiveness the following half an hour,
like a friend from childhood
it breathes on the shoulder or sleeps.

In the middle of the heatwave, it grabs the rose,
peels the pistachios,
or suddenly begins to stab.

A hand that had not yet dried up,
just a hand,
is the same one grooved by the bulldozer.

* * *

Three brothers are waiting for a frozen shirt on the
    clothesline.

TRAIN WHISTLE

I left my whole life there, thrown in unlocked closets,
dusty and neglected on the kitchen table along with
    painters' brochures.
I was not dying from happiness when for a second I thought
    I had the lifespan of plants
growing in the jungles of Africa
burning in a blink of an eye.

Meanwhile, the scents of places stayed engraved in my head
like a train whistle.

* * *

The house that I drew with plastic colours
had a chimney, a brown door, and a small window.
I hid it in the notebook dotted by our secretly shed tears.

Your nakedness is made visible by a star that fell on the
    rooftop.
We hide you between the cracks of the walls until the
    deer comes and takes you.
No stairs,
just your hand that pulls from their slumber those who
    drowned,
and your mouth that we want to kiss before the dawn.

Books explain why your body is the refuge of the birds,
and why the blinds never reach up to you:
we make love
for the first time
like we are going to die forever.

HERE AND THERE

My mother was there on the phone
and I was here far away from her
she asked me about my son and my wife and if I was
    all right
I reminded her of the past, the trees, and the rooftops . . .
I wanted her to laugh, and she laughed:

I was certain she spoke to me from the heart of darkness.

AMERICA'S POEMS

THE COAT ONLY

Close enough
You, miserable and intimate thing
that will not be just useless,
while you smile at the goddess wife,
in the borders which are slept in
by the description, slowly,
darkness in the streets
confuses you a lot
the coat only,
with its dangling buttons,
will bury the tilted head
of its owner:
—the head is like a dried fruit
bitten by a mouth
—the head with extreme agility
will fall on the shoulder of the man lying down
without a lifesaving rope.

SAN FRANCISCO'S WINDOW

Anything can almost happen:
—here, without a hat
you will wash your hands with a wide-open mouth
while listening to the groaning squirrel
that has been stuck in the brain since yesterday.
Then we open San Francisco's window
so you can see women taking off their clothes
at any time
they turn their waists towards the cloud:
the ship of all senses
made of ebony
moaning with a faint voice
lights up the lamps
for the bodies that dissolved in tears.

Anything can almost happen:
—here, without a hat
you will leave your house indefinitely.

ASPHALT

This world only misses one thing
which is a cork
that you stick in its behind
so it can sleep comfortably without its testicles,
or left on the edge of the river
like an empty bottle of beer.

And without a hint of regret
you will jump from the tenth floor
suffocated by too much air
that transformed into blood
as birds rest on the clean asphalt.

Dead birds
that no one pays attention to.

HI NEIGHBOUR

Good morning chair,
good morning stair,
in the street or at the house,
at the bar when the roof is wide and low
and the eyes staring at the door handle.

A cup of vodka is enough
for me to start a conversation with the walls
or with a waiter from Colombia
who crossed the border twenty years ago,
then married an American woman older than his mother.

'Hi neighbour' with a wave of a hand
no one in America would say that
except for the crazy Dutchman next door.

He used to live in the same district
where I currently live . . .
the same street

Here, he wrote 'Howl' in Paterson
crowded with Black and Spanish people
Arabs and marijuana
He died like John the Baptist
while swimming in beer and insulin.

No one was with him
when he walked up the New Jersey stairs
then threw himself
under the seven o'clock train.

A LIGHT CLOUD OUTSIDE THE NOTE

On Broadway
I am listening to jazz
and the cut-off necks near the counter pass
the hanging face looks like a burnt lamp
the abrupt face
would be enough to stay like that
after it gets carried by the saxophone
a light cloud outside the note
and nothing is left of it
beside the drawing of a shadow on the wall.

On Broadway
I cannot forget about taxes and the monthly rent,
love, marriage, and phone bills,
which I did not yet pay in full
I will definitely remember it.

From the Main Street
to Prospect Park
I turn the key in the door's lock
entering the house with a dizzy head
and wet pants.

On Broadway
I will cruise down Broadway in a 1987 Cadillac,
with a broken window on the driver's side

and the antifreeze dripping
from the radiator.

A car that moans
or catches its last breaths,
I loved it like it was a person
between us is a longstanding intimacy

like a house
guarded by the picture of a father who never smiles.

THE GREEN MOON

In Hollywood
Jennifer Lopez gave me a kiss
on my right cheek
Oh God! I will never forget it.

In Hollywood
where I do not dare to wander
its street
in fear of stumbling upon Sylvester Stallone
carrying his plastic machine gun
and his vengeful laugh
at his enemies

In Hollywood
I will shout:
—I am Antonio Banderas
in *The Green Moon*.

The last blink of an eye around the top of the bottle
that I bought from a 'spiritual' liquor store
in New York,
'Our Price 15.99' was written on it.

Youssef Bazzi will not save me here
from what I am dealing with now,
and he did not know that the last cup was white,
completely white
like this table
that Edgar Allan Poe sits on
it will definitely vanish soon.

The last cup I got right
before it reached its due date
under 'the roof':

'Goodbye Golsari?'

Antonio said to me:
'I read the work of a poet from Egypt in Spanish
his name is Ahmed Adaweyah
and I love a song
by an Egyptian artist too
his name is Ahmed Abdelmu'ti Hejazi
I have friends from Turkey, Syria,
and Lebanon . . .

This guy Antonio
cannot stop from spinning around
and drinking margaritas
and chasing fat women.

He always imagines himself riding a horse
between mountains,
unable to sleep
wearing his cane hat.

NAMES OF CITIES

Names of cities
my heart certainly does not beat to them,
humans, on their shoulders
are fixing them with nails.

Widows,
sick people,
the strong desire in joints
and the sweat that seeps profusely from the statues.

Names of cities
that I offered to you, including their red and yellow Indians
and phones that ring without wires
—I want a coat this winter
and a ride back home
even if on a broken train.

Like Chicago at dawn
I am Charles the Fifth who is incapable of sleep
I am Columbus' muse,
spots of blood stuck between his teeth.
On the shelf, your statue stands, its dignity wounded

It is not strange
to remind you of the thirteen years
that were longer than Walt Whitman's beard
during the Middle Ages
in Damascus's museums
and Castile's kingdom that I built for you
under the grapevine.

It is not strange
that I sit in Central Park, lonely,
and I have nothing to lose,
the Bohemians will change the spots they sleep in
then quickly drink their soup
and not shower
as long as they are smoking their weed.

It is not strange
that you were alarmed
and the visitor to the house whose visit turned out heavy
    on the host.

In case of loneliness
in a land that does not belong to anyone
fighters ignore the language of its residents.

You are half-submerged in water until mid-afternoon
no bird's wing has touched you
and no guard stayed to guard you.

Any man would see the perfectness of his lineage
the moment he goes down barefoot
to your mysterious thing.

Any stranger
owns his heart when he passes by in the house
and would not inform you about the wedding bed.

Any conversation with horses
so that the shepherds suddenly understand the secret of
    your open door
after dawn.

BECAUSE HE IS YOUR DELICATE ENEMY

In vain
the one falling from your eyes
has a sister from photographs
and relatives who live in the night
without a wolf guarding their shivers during the cold

Using water, you bring out the wild beasts
from the stone and the body
because it is naked and the gaze has washed it
that is stripped towards the wilderness
the day is clear

Because he is your kind enemy
and your lover with a bad reputation.

Those running away towards the roofs of your houses
could not sleep

Their rifles, bones, and perforated hats
fell like a fistful of salt
on the same ground where you took
the man in your arms
and they have five children
and scars drawn under the eyes

The escapers
for all of that
they slipped heading in your direction, accompanied by
    the Armenians
and the Kurds from the mountains, the Circassians, and
    the Assyrians
and Indians from Delaware and the Berbers
so each of them could find the stranger in his family

The stranger that was hidden
by the thigh extended on the sand.

INFECTED WITH LEPROSY

Let them come forward one after another
to describe the bird on your right
the musicians get you and the tears are filled
with the smell of your clothes

About nakedness in Jerusalem
and the wall that the goddess of writing
leaned upon

About the boy who married you the second time
for your very expensive pelvis
and he did not tell his mother
that he'd reached puberty.

Let them come forward where there is no need to explain
    the vanity
that surrounds the gardens of the reigning system.

The more handsome among them takes you east of Jordan
the one infected with leprosy
you make him grow up in two years.

AFTER MIDNIGHT

He takes you to his house in the basement
to be with you for the whole night
with an eye to committing a crime
he is able to touch the corner of the air
on your lower lip
or the cloud on your breasts.

Lying down on a soft black mattress
not surrendering to the thirst
or losing his path.

After midnight
ripped off your tree
he can love you intensely
trembling with vulnerability.